*A collection of my favourite thoughts
& tools with the intention to empower*

Written by Maree Gatt

Illustrated by Ayesha Dharmabandu

First published by Busybird Publishing 2021

Copyright © 2021 Maree Gatt

ISBN:

978-1-922465-73-3 (paperback)
978-1-922465-74-0 (hardback)
978-1-922465-75-7 (ebook)

This work is copyright. Apart from any use permitted under the *Copyright Act 1968*, no part of this publication may be reproduced, stored in a retrieval system or transmitted in any form or by any means, electronic, mechanical, photocopying, recording or otherwise, without the prior written permission of Maree Gatt.

Cover Image: Ayesha Dharmabandu

Cover design: Busybird Publishing

Layout and typesetting: Busybird Publishing

Illustrations: Ayesha Dharmabandu

Busybird Publishing
2/118 Para Road
Montmorency, Victoria
Australia 3094
www.busybird.com.au

Dedicated to all those I have crossed paths with:
Your lessons have been transformed into wisdom.

Contents

Preface	1
Feeling Stuck	7
Resilience	9
Anxiety	11
Vibration	13
Uncomfortable Comfort Zone	15
Polarity	17
Sacred Frequencies	19
Manage Your Robot	21
Agenda	23
Contentment	25
Ripple Effect	27
Inner Strength	29
Journey Of Life	31
Be Real	33
God	35
Tag You're It	37
Start Now	39
Your Schedule	41
Understand But Don't Always Accept	43
Core Beliefs	45
Swapsies	47
Boundaries	49
Change	51
Narcissist Hunter	53
Fight Or Flight	55
From Heroes To Superheroes	57
Love	59

Objectivity	61
Transform	63
Replace	65
Reflection	67
Purpose	69
Power	71
Faith	73
Addiction	75
Cool. Calm. Collected	77
Grounding	79
Sacred Pieces Of Shit	81
Let Go Of Hurt	83
Victim Mentality	85
Perception	87
Chemicals	89
Karmic Relationships	91
Closure	93
Listen	95
Suffering	97
Just Chill	99
Challenge It	101
Adulthood	103
Own Your Shit	105
Nothing Is Solid	107
Mental Gymnastics	109
You	111
Organised Chaos	113
Love Prevails	117
Acknowledgements	119
Disclaimer	121
About The Author	123
About The Illustrator	125

Preface

My name is Maree and I am a Clinical Psychologist and Reiki Practitioner; working and living in Melbourne, Australia. I run a small business called Peace By Piece Psychology, where I have the privilege of doing what I love, helping and assisting people to work through any struggles that may be preventing them from being their truest self. I love my job, in fact from a very young age I found myself always observing those around me, fascinated with their mannerisms, body language, and associated behaviours. I then decided to dedicate my life to learning and understanding the human psyche. I love helping people work through the blocks that inhibit their ability to reach their full potential. Every person I chat to has a story worth telling and I learn and gain so much from these conversations. I have a keen eye for observation and a drive to dive into the minds of those around me. I love attempting to really understand the core of peoples' existence and understanding the agendas that drive their behaviours. I also have a deep love for the universe and all that it encompasses. It's through this eternal understanding, that I have learnt to understand the urge for unity that our souls crave, and it's through my work that I get to help people achieve this in a practical sense. It's through my work and several life experiences, that I have gained the privilege of understanding many walks of life… but through it all, what I have noticed is that even though we are all so unique, we still suffer from the same shitty life situations. I often see patterns in behaviour and personalities that demonstrate to me that the fundamental core of each of us is similar. We all just want to be loved and happy, but unfortunately our life experiences and various traumas distract us from the simplicity of achieving this.

In 2016, I decided to start my own private practice and really use this platform as a way to honestly just… spread the love… and give each person the opportunity to explore their inner demons and have the opportunity to potentially set those demons free.

I think the most valuable thing is being raw and authentic, that's my style. I'm just me and

I like to think that I am a very down to earth person serving information on a very honest plate. I think if you can learn from experiences and then use those lessons to help assist others, then that gives you the ability for much personal growth. By assisting and showing compassion for just one other person, you are then creating a potential ripple effect that will gradually spread across humanity. If one piece of helpful information can in some way improve someone's quality of life, then that's a win to me. Based on this, I decided to put together this book, which highlights some of my thoughts, understandings, quotes, and ideas that I think people would really benefit from.

This isn't a self-help book but a bunch of ideas that I would love nothing more than to share with as many people who are willing to give it a read. I see a common lack of understanding on the principles of the universe and how these themes should be interpreted. Furthermore, I see a basic lack of understanding of the self and at times this disconnect from self-awareness and lack of insight can cause the most damage of all. I think inner wisdom is a power tool that we should all strive for, as it has provided me with nothing but knowledge and peace. My idea for this book is to provide a very easy, raw, authentic and simplified way to understand oneself and the amazing universe that we are all connected to. There is something in this book for everyone and I touch on a vast range of themes. I encourage you to hold an open mind, but more importantly, an open heart.

My idea is that this little gift will be a helpful handbook for everyone and some of the proceeds made on the book will be donated to charity. I have chosen the Australian Childhood Foundation as I absolutely love what they represent and do. They are dedicated to helping traumatised children recover from the devastating impact of abuse, neglect, and family violence. I am a huge advocate for early intervention and I truly believe that if we provide the right support to children who have been the victims of childhood trauma, then this will potentially help prevent them from experiencing significant mental health issues when they are older.

My aim for 'Shades of Being' is for it to reach as many people as possible, providing some form of wisdom, understanding, or support for that person, which then will enable them to continue that positive ripple effect for the rest of humanity. I just want to share the love.

So, grab a coffee, chuck your feet up, get comfy, and let's explore the many shades of being!

~Feeling Stuck~

Often, we convince ourselves to stay in a situation that we know instinctively is not right for us. The more we stay in that situation, the more exhausted and unhappier we feel. Your body will tell you when something or someone is detrimental to your health. Don't force yourself to remain in a place that inhibits your happiness and growth, never let fear of the unknown stop you from walking away from a situation that no longer serves a positive purpose in your life. If you have to constantly do mental gymnastics to convince yourself that you are happy in a situation, then that situation potentially doesn't align with your higher purpose. Sometimes the best things in life happen right after we decide to steer away from a situation and embark on a new journey.

You cannot heal in the same environment that made you sick

- Erico Mesiano.

~ Resilience ~

Learn to bounce back from turmoil. Things won't always go your way, but don't get defeated! It's after the comeback that you reach the most amazing places! Learn to not give up and believe that no matter what, you can overcome all of life's obstacles. Life is the game and resilience is your weapon!

~Anxiety~

Anxiety is one of the most common psychological conditions that people present with. Anxiety is basically fear associated with the unknown, a sense of lack of control or being in danger, and a basic feeling of uncertainty about the future. Those fears often manifest into hypervigilant physical symptoms that leave people feeling confused and defeated. One of the most important things when feeling this way is to regulate your nervous system. When we feel anxious we naturally start to take shallow breathes which limits proper oxygen flow through our bodies. Learning to breathe properly helps to calm your nervous system, therefore easing the symptoms you might be experiencing.

4-7-8 breathing is a breathing technique developed by Dr. Andrew Weil which will help calm the nervous system:

- ◊ Breathe in for 4 seconds
- ◊ Hold your breath for 7 seconds
- ◊ Breathe out slowly for 8 seconds

~ Vibration ~

The human body is made up of trillions of cells, all which vibrate. Everything and everyone have a certain vibration, the frequency of existence. The higher the vibration, the healthier the cell. Negative experiences and emotions vibrate on a much lower and dense level, whereas more positive experiences and emotions vibrate on a much higher frequency. Whatever level you are vibrating on, that's the level of vibration in all things that you will attract. Our thoughts may send out things like "I will fail" or "I am angry" and then our emotions will then respond to those thoughts by drawing into our lives an event to match that emotional frequency. Happiness and joy attract happiness and joy. Sadness and fear attract sadness and fear. Your thoughts will determine your emotional frequency, so have a think about how you can change the way you think and feel so that you can harvest the experiences that you want!

Aim to think, feel, and vibe high!

~Uncomfortable Comfort Zone~

One of the common traits in people who are unhappy is their tendency to remain in a situation that no longer serves them. I call this an *uncomfortable comfort zone.* The longer we stay in this zone of comfort, the more we feel unsatisfied. Sometimes we need to stop focusing on what isn't working and start thinking about what needs to happen to reignite your zest for life. Stop accepting that your uncomfortable comfort zone is your reality and start working towards a life that you're satisfied with. If you don't know where to begin, answering the following questions may be a helpful start:

> When did you feel the most excited and motivated? When in your life did you feel happy? What was it that made this a really good period in your life?

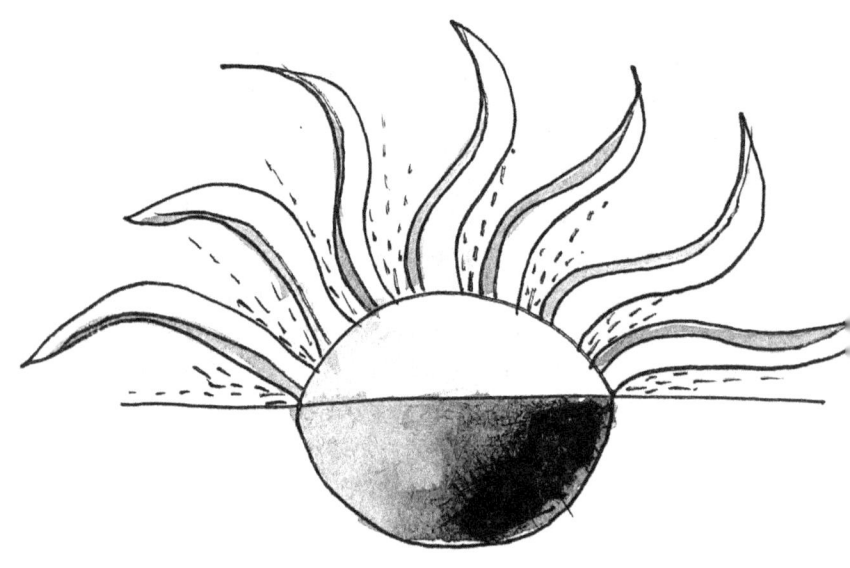

~ Polarity ~

Everything in life has an opposite, that is the law of polarity. Darkness & light, positive & negative, and love & hate. Everything is on a continuum and life is different vibrational experiences on this continuum. Without the darkness there would be no appreciation for the light because from this darkness the light was created. Use the dark moments in your life to push you towards growth and understanding and use the that growth to understand the need for the darkness that you experienced. If you only recognise the light you will not learn and if you only recognise the dark there will be no progression and growth. This is why it is important to embrace polarity. Create a life that encompasses this balance.

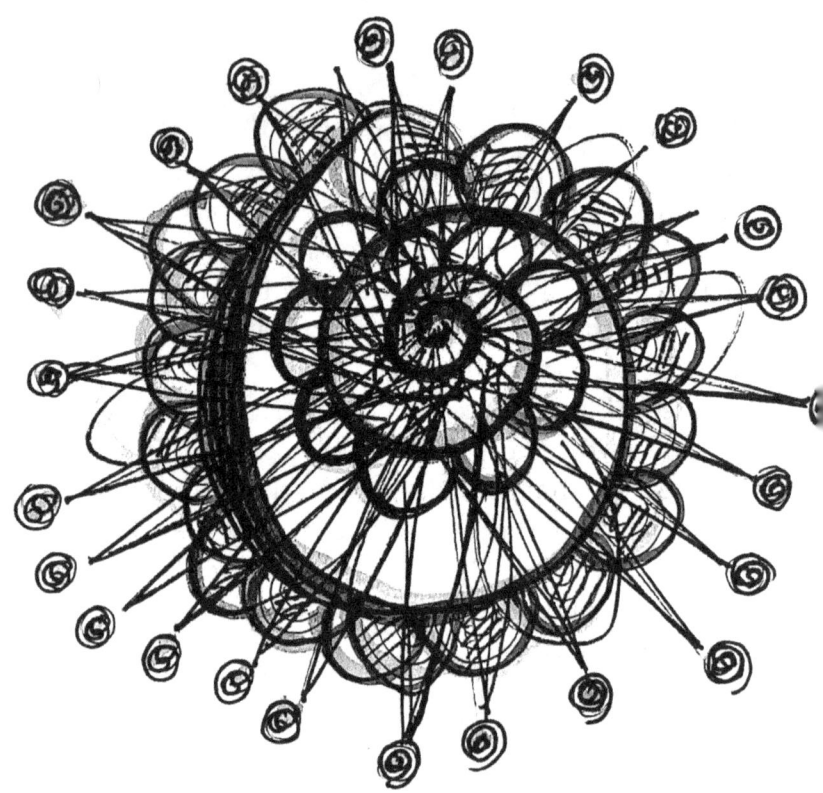

~Sacred Frequencies~

A simple way to calm inner turmoil is to complete a sound meditation that compliments the frequency of that problem and helps to restore peace within the body. Our vibration is constantly changing and using these sacred frequencies can help restore love, peace, balance, and contentment.

Use the following Solfeggio frequencies for each stated problem (you can find each of these by simply searching for them on YouTube).

> 174 Hertz → Alleviates pain
> 283 Hertz → Heals tissue and targets body energy field
> 396 Hertz → Releases fear and guilt
> 417 Hertz → Facilitates change and boosts creativity
> 432 Hertz → Miracle tone of nature
> 528 Hertz → Brings about transformation and miracles by restructuring DNA to perfect form
> 639 Hertz → Heals relationships
> 741 Hertz → Awakens intuition, empowerment, and self confidence
> 852 Hertz → Attracts soul tribe and reconnects you with spiritual order
> 963 Hertz → Connects with light and spirit

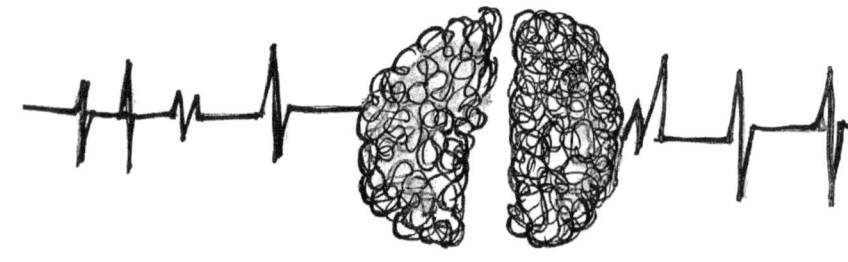

~ Manage Your Robot ~

Never underestimate the power of your thoughts! Your body is a slave to your mind. What your mind sees, your body feels … your body is a robot with your mind in complete control. Perception is everything; what you think, you become! Learn to understand those repetitive thoughts that may be causing your body to always feel tense. Stop thinking yourself into a shit space, you are in complete control of that, no one else. Your imagination becomes reality, so think wisely!

~Agenda~

People can be complicated and ambiguous, but there is a little strategy that you can employ that will help you better understand a person's agenda.

Sometimes we need to look beyond one's behaviour and work out the hidden agenda driving that behaviour. Peoples actions don't always coincide with what they are trying to accomplish. Hidden agendas are self-serving but they don't always have to be malicious in nature (e.g. pushing someone away when fundamentally you don't want them to abandon you). You will find that when you focus on what is actually driving one's behaviour and not just the behaviour they're presenting with, then you will understand that person or their future behaviour more thoroughly.

The trick here though, is to learn about ulterior motives with an open and non-judgemental mind.

~Contentment~

Maybe the aim in life is not happiness, as that is a temporary emotion like sadness, anger, or feeling excited. Working towards always being happy is unrealistic and these high expectations always set us up for failure. Maybe the aim in life is to feel content. This state is achievable and means that no matter where you are at in life, you can always feel at peace.

~ Ripple Effect ~

Your purpose in life should be to create a ripple effect. Helping improve the life of one person, then leads to a better life for those around them, causing a beautiful snowball effect for generations to come. This may mean that certain experiences will need to take place in one's life to deepen their understanding of human nature to create awareness and compassion. Materialistic things only have monetary value and the gains are short lived, but leaving a legacy that creates more peace and happiness for generations to come … now that lasts longer than a lifetime!

~ Inner Strength ~

Sometimes life throws at you the most difficult and disruptive curve balls and you have no choice but to rely on your inner strength to pull you through. Be thankful for the blessing of inner strength, because through this, you will then be able to remind others that they too can handle anything that is thrown their way. So here is a little reminder that situations are only temporary and you should not feel defeated as your inner strength will pull you through. Resilience will turn you into a warrior in life, the type of warrior with unconquerable will that empowers others to never give up!

There is a Japanese proverb called *'Nana korob, ya oki'* which translates to *'fall seven times, but stand up eight'*. I think this proverb perfectly highlights the importance of inner strength and its role in helping us to not give up no matter how hard we fall.

~Journey Of Life~

Life can be compared to one big train ride with many stops. Sometimes we stay at a stop for much longer than others and some stops are only very temporary. The point is that all stops are necessary stops that are part of our journey to that one destination. Be patient at all stops that seem to last a little longer, enjoy those very short intense stops, but most of all, just embrace your own unique journey. Life is about the experience and not just the destination.

~Be Real~

A common discomfort in people is their inability to comfortably live in their own reality. Many of us tend to create illusions based on our egos, desires, insecurities, and then attempt to convince ourselves that these illusions are our authentic experiences. When these distorted projections are made, it then tends to manifest into anxiety, depression, and helplessness. Knowledge and experience are ambiguous as they are open ended and based on our own perceptions; thus, our version of reality can become an illusion. It's very important to own your shit and be true to yourself. Stop attempting to deceive yourself because you fear the real YOU. The real you is fundamentally a good and peaceful being, however complicated by the bullshit you have gone through.

~God~

Maybe we all know of the same truth, but we just translate it in different languages. We all relate to music, but we prefer to listen to it in different beats and rhythms. Maybe our understanding of God is the same… all religions and beliefs are fundamentally communicating the same message, just in different ways.

My truth is all about consciousness and connectedness, without one, you cannot have the other.

~Tag You're It~

Challenges are what makes life interesting, and overcoming them is what makes life meaningful. Experience it, own it, learn from it, then pass it on! TAG … you're it!

~Start Now~

You just have to keep moving forward. Start where you are now, start with fear, start with doubt. Start and don't stop. Start where you are and with what you have.

- *Ijeoma Umebinyou*

You can't wait for the day for things to improve, you have to get up and start the process with whatever energy and resources you have. Just … start … now!

~Your Schedule~

Don't beat yourself up for where you are now! Stop comparing where you are at in life with those around you, we are all on very different schedules!

The experiences in your life are all part of your own unique journey, so embrace wherever you are at on that journey.

You are exactly where you need to be and nothing is off schedule.

- Emily Maroutian

~Understand But Don't Always Accept~

Just because you understand someone's behaviour, that doesn't mean you have to accept it. It is important to understand someone's hardship and reasoning behind their behaviour, but don't let that be an excuse for them to disrespect you and violate your boundaries. Empathy is a beautiful quality to have but don't let it influence you to make excuses for someone else's shitty behaviour. Otherwise, you will resent the fact that you are an empathetic person and it will shut you down. Love and embrace your empathetic side, but be wise in who you choose to direct that attention to. It is not your responsibility to pacify another's dysfunctional behaviour.

~Core Beliefs~

Core beliefs are those fundamental and sometimes annoying beliefs we develop as a young child. If you track your negative thoughts for a while, you will be able to identify patterns in them. When we group these thoughts into patterns, we then come to core beliefs. Of course, these beliefs can be irrational as they were developed through a child's perspective. If they remain in your subconscious without awareness, then they start to interfere with your perspective and ability to read situations for what they truly are. Learn the difference between a conscious thought and a subconscious thought influenced by a core belief.

~Swapsies~

Whenever you are feeling an unsettling emotion such as sad, angry, or stressed, do something that makes you feel the opposite emotion. Deposit that negative emotion into its opposite positive emotion! If you are feeling sad, go and do something that makes you feel happy! Feeling anxious? Then go and do something that helps you chill the hell out!

SAD	→	HAPPY
ANGRY	→	CALM
STRESS	→	RELAXED

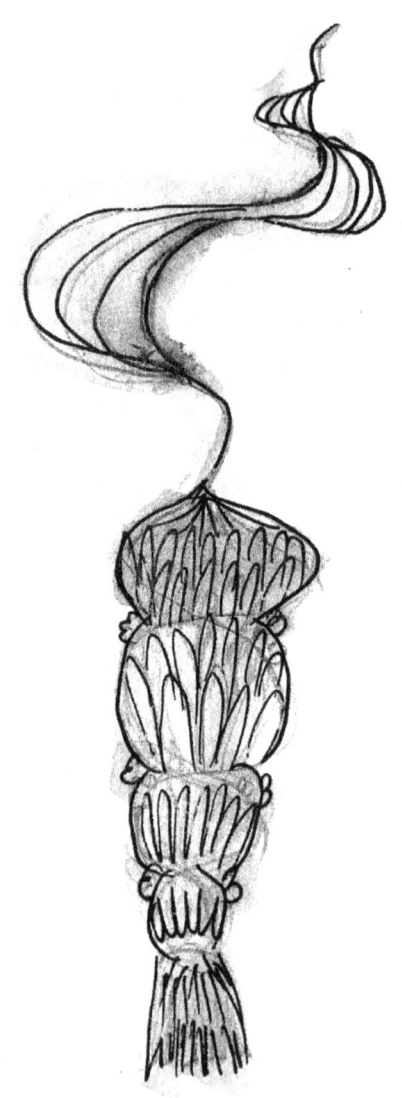

~Boundaries~

Boundaries … by far, are the most important thing that everyone needs to develop! We live in a world surrounded by people who are intentional or unintentional energy vampires. Learn to say no, learn to say you don't like something, learn to screen people before you trust them, learn to make sure you are ok before you go and try to rescue someone else. If you don't, then you are basically walking around with a tattoo on your forehead saying "Take advantage of me", and it will be those energy vampires that will be reading it. Once this dysfunctional bond is made, you will potentially be left feeling exhausted, depleted, and helpless.

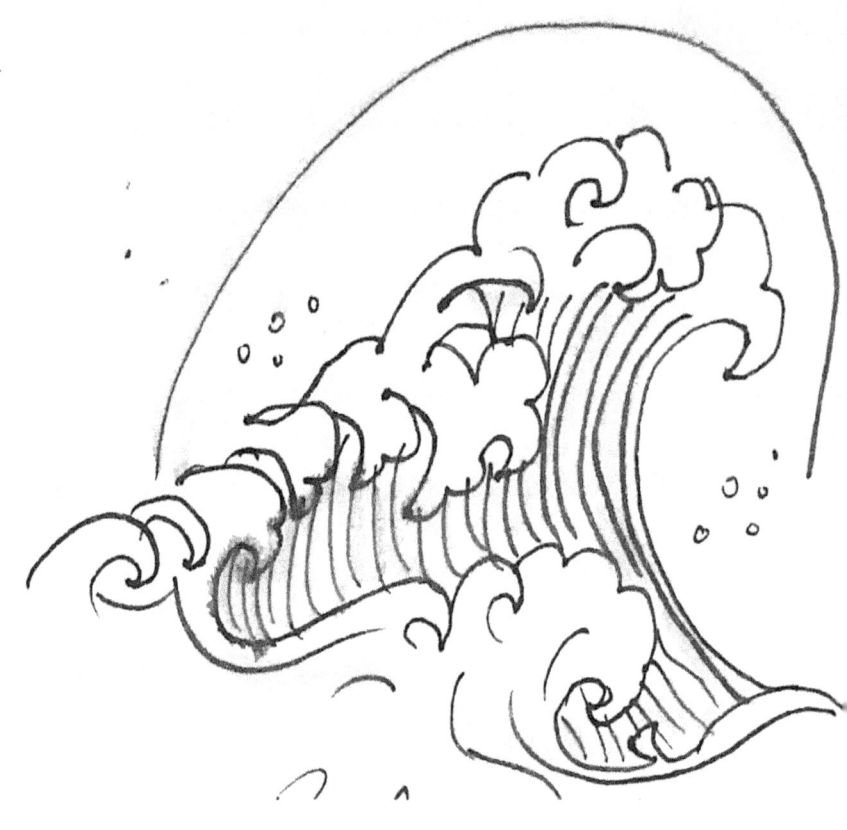

~Change~

The only thing that is really ever certain in life is change. Situations evolve and pass, attachment to certain material things dissipates, people that we love pass away, friends you thought would be there move on, relationships that broke your heart seem to transform into a lesson, your favourite moments become distant memories, the seasons continue to change, and you continue to get older. Change is the only certainty in life, embracing it and rolling with the punches is our biggest mission yet.

~Narcissist Hunter~

Narcissism, a concept that gets thrown around regularly. Sadly, there are many victims of narcissistic abuse. Learn to identify the tell-tale signs that these individuals present so that you can avoid becoming too emotionally involved with them. If someone appears way too good to be true and it's not sitting right within you, then tune into that feeling and question their motives.

Here are a few traits to look out for:

- ◊ Highly manipulative
- ◊ Sensitive to physical appearance
- ◊ Oversensitive to criticism
- ◊ Others are always to blame
- ◊ Seek validation
- ◊ Very charming
- ◊ Vindictive
- ◊ Control freaks
- ◊ Feel no empathy
- ◊ Fragile ego

~Fight Or Flight~

Life is full of stress that triggers the nervous system. The human body evolved to be able to deal with bursts of stress as they occur. If ancestral man was chased by a vicious animal, his body would experience a huge amount of stress, but only for a short period of time. The human body is designed to deal with stress quickly and then return back to a normal level of functioning, which we call homeostasis. Stress in 21st century living is entirely different and something our bodies are not designed to cope with (e.g. anxiety from mortgage repayments, divorce, serious illness, or financial problems). We are not designed to deal with these events and the prolonged stress that they create. We have to learn to manage this stress more effectively so that our nervous systems don't take a beating every time we feel some level of stress. Some good ways to manage this stress would be through breathing exercises, meditation, physical exercise, being in nature, getting a massage, and any other healthy coping strategy.

~From Heroes To Superheroes~

There comes a point in your life when you realise your parents are no longer just 'Heroes', where you understand your parents are only human with their own issues to deal with. They have their own set of insecurities, struggles, and difficulties. It's like you start to feel emotionally older and understand things in much more depth. It's at this point that you love them even more, because you can appreciate all that they have done for you despite their own inner struggles. It's through this observation, that you may not see them as the original heroes you thought they were, but rather as superheroes. Understanding their resilience then helps you to grow emotionally and shake off any intergenerational grief or trauma so that you can then decide on your own fate!

~ *Love* ~

Love shouldn't be hard, it should be easy, it should flow, it should calm you. Don't confuse the butterflies you get in your stomach during an intense relationship, with those you get when excited by love. Those intense relationships that feel like an emotional roller coaster trigger butterflies in your stomach not due to excitement, but due to anxiety. In this case, the relationship has triggered your instincts and is manifesting in symptoms of anxiety. Inconsistent, unpredictable, uncertain love, makes the body feel restless … real, unconditional, authentic love, will calm your body and make you feel at ease.

~ Objectivity ~

Master objectivity. Do not let yourself be affected or controlled by what others say and do. You are the only person who is in control of your feelings, if you let others affect you, then you let them control you. You have to get to a point where your mood does not shift based on the actions of those around you. Sit back and learn to observe things around you with logic. Allow your character to be fuelled with observation, understanding, and objectivity.

~ Transform ~

Flip any difficult life experience into consciously improving yourself and guiding those around you. Don't waste your past traumas on repetitive sorrow and negativity, use them to transform the world around you. Become an alchemist.

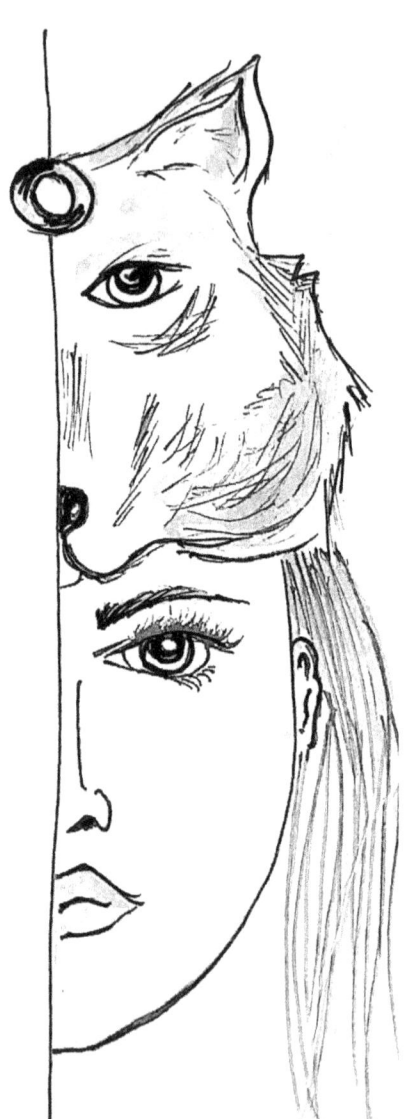

~ Replace ~

Humans… creatures of habit. We tend to do the same behaviour but expect a different result. Change only happens when you actively choose to drop old, unhealthy habits and bounce into new, promising healthy habits! If you are unsure where to start, try by replacing some of these common bad habits with the suggested healthier ones:

Instead of over thinking, try some mindfulness.

Instead of focusing on the problem, start thinking about some solutions.

Instead of being negative, try and think about things you are thankful for.

Instead of staying up late, get a good night's sleep.

Instead of worrying about completing many tasks, just focus on one thing at a time.

Instead of investing your time into toxic people, start surrounding yourself with people who inspire you.

Instead of overusing T.V and devices, focus more on your hobbies and being active.

Instead of always being in victim mentality, start taking responsibility for your own emotions and behaviours.

Instead of eating chocolate, still have the chocolate! It's bloody good for the soul!

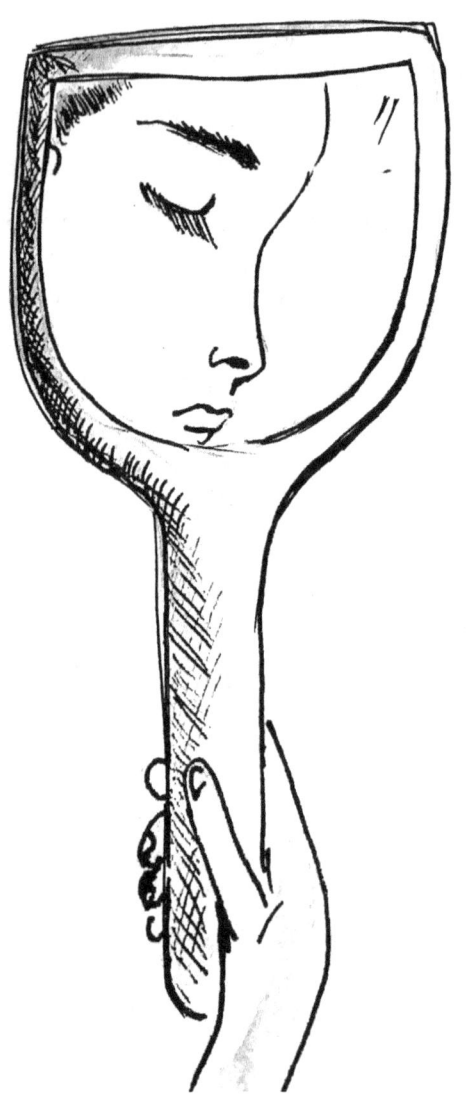

~ Reflection ~

What bothers you the most about other people? What qualities do you admire in them? The way we evaluate others is not just about the characteristics we observe, it's actually a reflection of our own insecurities or strengths. How we react towards others and the things we react to, may suggest something about ourselves that we have been ignoring. Once we learn to observe and understand this concept, we then gain the most amazing awareness about ourselves so that we can then initiate positive change.

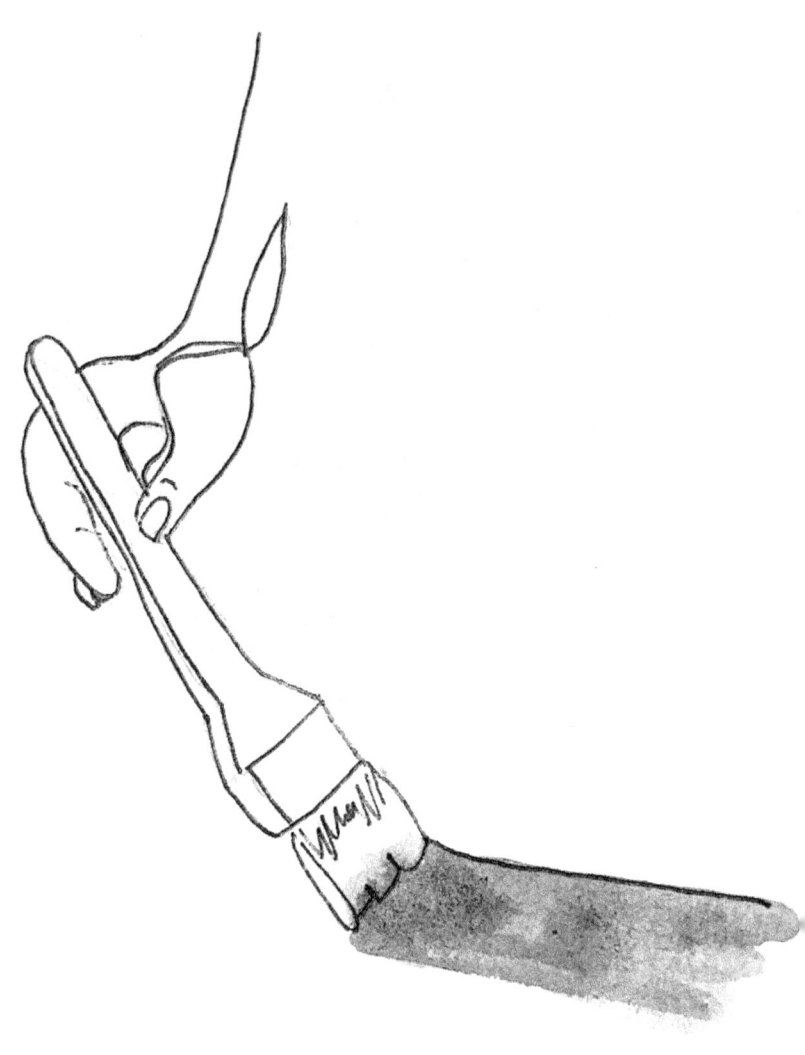

~ Purpose ~

*The mystery of human existence lies not in just staying alive,
but in finding something to live for*

- Fyodor Dostoyevsky.

When one feels as though they have a lack of purpose in this world, self-sabotaging behaviour is sure to follow. There is no greater discomfort than not living out the true potential of your soul.

If you find it difficult to understand your purpose, then shift the focus towards whatever makes you feel passionate! It is within this enthusiasm of your passion that you will be directed to the essence of your true purpose.

If you love creating, then build!

If you love to nurture, then help others!

If you love to mentor, then teach!

If you love excitement, then go on adventures!

If you love to learn, then study!

If you love solitude, then embrace the silence!

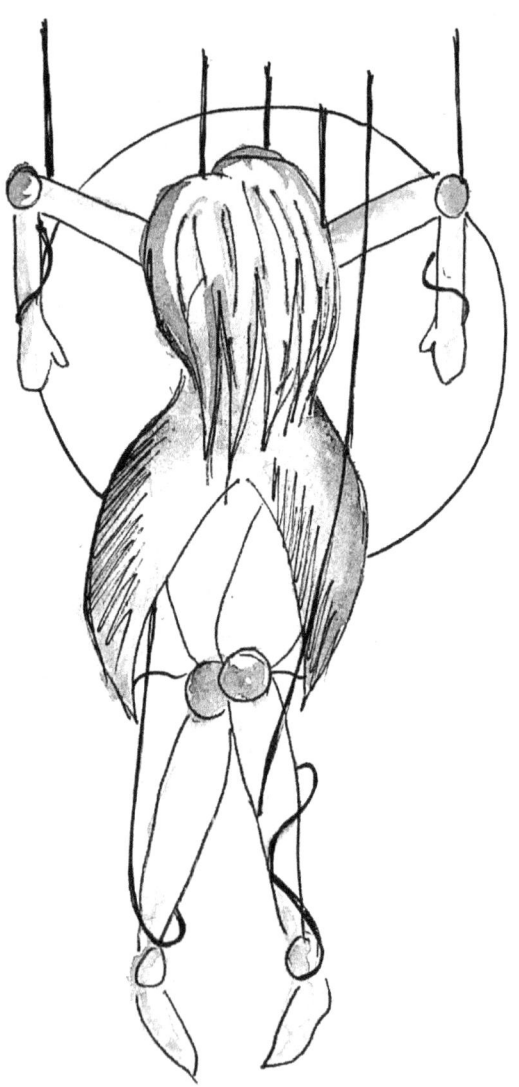

~ Power ~

True power does not come from controlling others, it actually comes from an ability to manage your own emotional reactions to situations and those that may trigger you.
You will continue to be distressed if you allow yourself to emotionally react to everything that is said and done to you. True power comes from being able to maintain your own inner emotional state, despite the stress around you. Breathe and just allow things to pass!

True power is sitting back and observing things with magic.
True power is restraint.

- *Warren Buffett*

~ Faith ~

Have faith in your vision, hold it close. Remember what you set out to do, remember the way you need to go. Manoeuvre around barriers that may get in your way. Trust the process.
In all chaos there is a secret order that we are sometimes blind to. Welcome the uncertainty, embrace the change. When you finally get there, you will discover that nothing in life is ever random.

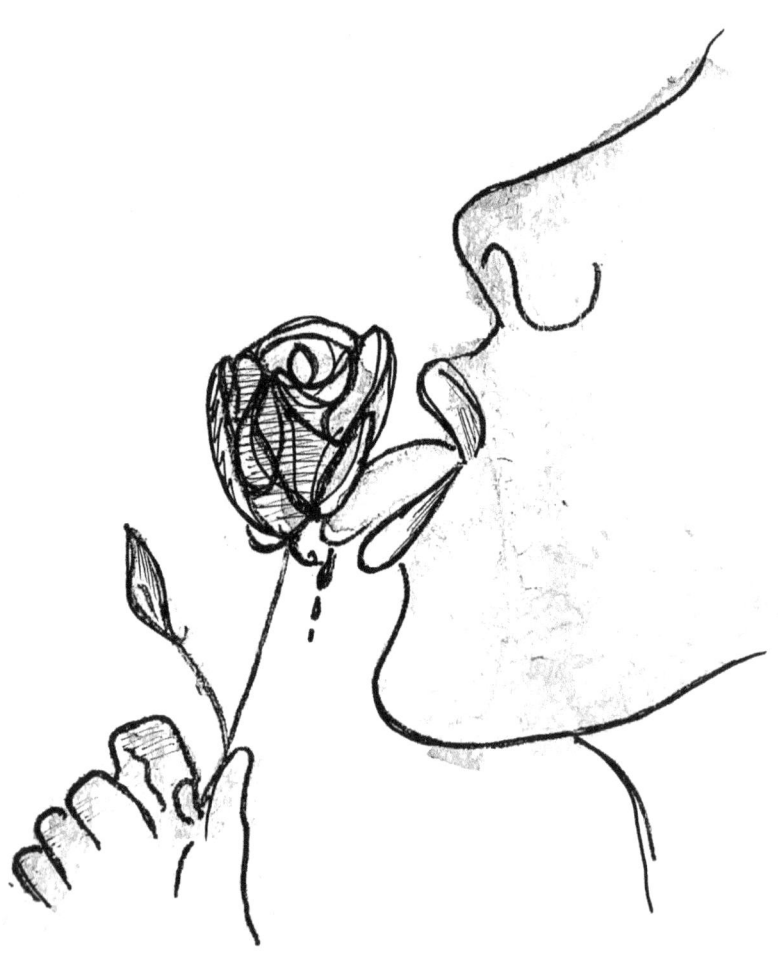

~Addiction~

Drugs, alcohol, gambling, food, shopping, sex, or even co-dependent relationships … whatever your drug of choice is, the biggest problem is a lack of belief in the self to cope. Commonly, people become attached to their addictions that they can no longer see themselves as separate to their addiction. Truth is, the addiction is kind of like a toxic and manipulative best mate who has always been there, but who has slowly chipped away at your self-confidence and perceptions around your ability to manage your problems. Building healthier coping strategies and perceptions of the self are vital for anyone who is battling with letting go of their addiction. Everything you ever need or want, you can truly find within yourself.

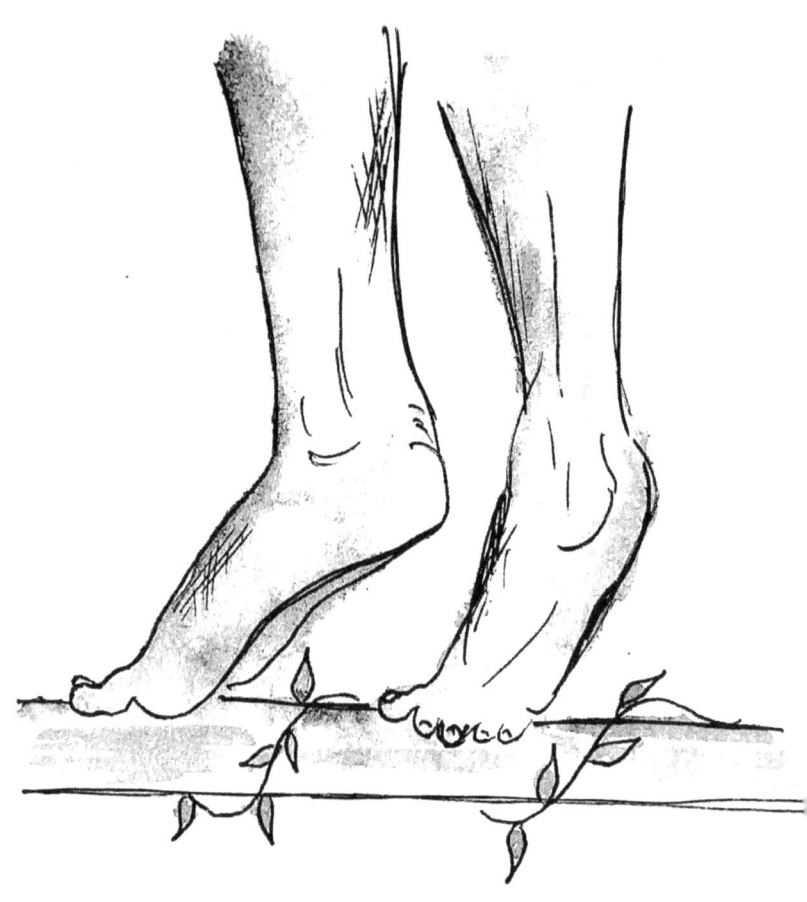

~Cool. Calm. Collected~

People are always going to have something to say about what you are doing. Don't let that deter you, as their perception potentially may illustrate their own inadequacies. The choices made based on your own convictions will lead to personal growth and eventually, success. Always own your shit without deflection or denial. Maintain composure, stay well respected, cool, calm, and always collected.

~Grounding~

Sometimes we can get stuck in our minds, feeling disconnected from ourselves and the world around us. When you are feeling this disconnect, go into your backyard, take your socks and shoes off, put your bare feet on the grass and just focus on the feeling of the earth beneath your feet. Nature is SO healing, we just have to tune into its beautiful frequency.

~Sacred Pieces Of Shit~

We are all sacred, nothing more, nothing less. We all have an ego. We all have the capacity to empower and to be empowered. We can all be selfish, yet be selfless. We can all lie, yet expect honesty in return. We can all chase greed, yet give to the hungry. We are all powerful beings who sometimes just lose our way.

We are all sacred, yet also at times, pieces of shit.

~Let Go Of Hurt~

Always allow yourself to feel your hurt fully. Close your eyes, observe the energy that you feel in your body when you reflect on the hurt. Once you have identified that place, breathe air into it and send love and calmness to that particular sensation. Allow that empty feeling to be replaced with love.

~ Victim Mentality ~

Victim mentality is stubborn, it is the inability for someone to distance themselves from their past traumas. People with this mentality tend to constantly see themselves as victims which keeps them constantly looping around their trauma and looking for ways to reinforce their traumatised self.

The thing is, it's important to take responsibility for the way you are feeling now, you can't change your past, but you can decide how you feel about it now. Instead of sitting in victim mentality, work on improving your willpower as this is necessary to create a positive shift and help change your responses to your emotions. Take responsibility from this moment forward and have the willpower to not give in to old victimised thought patterns.

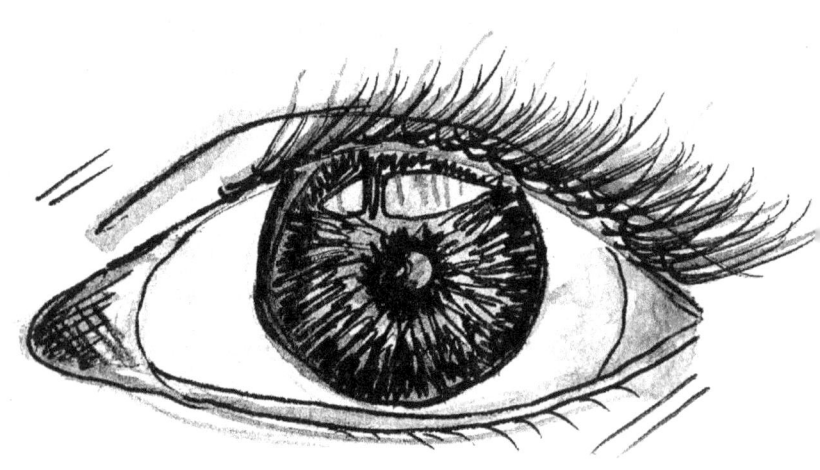

~ Perception ~

Perception really is everything. Our perception is based on our imagination and information being filtered through our own values, experiences, and beliefs. Once information has been processed through these individual filters, the reality of the situation is often lost in translation.

Sometimes we look in the mirror and only see the negative in the reflection looking back at us. Don't waste your dreams and potential on that one reflection you see, as again, your perception is everything! The version of yourself that you see, is the version of yourself that you will project out to the world. If you see fear, you will demonstrate fear. If you see dissatisfaction, you will be dissatisfied.

Learn to navigate through those preconceived beliefs that you have developed and start to see the amazing and powerful being that you are. If you see courage, you will be courageous; If you see acceptance, you will learn to accept. If you see love, you will demonstrate love.

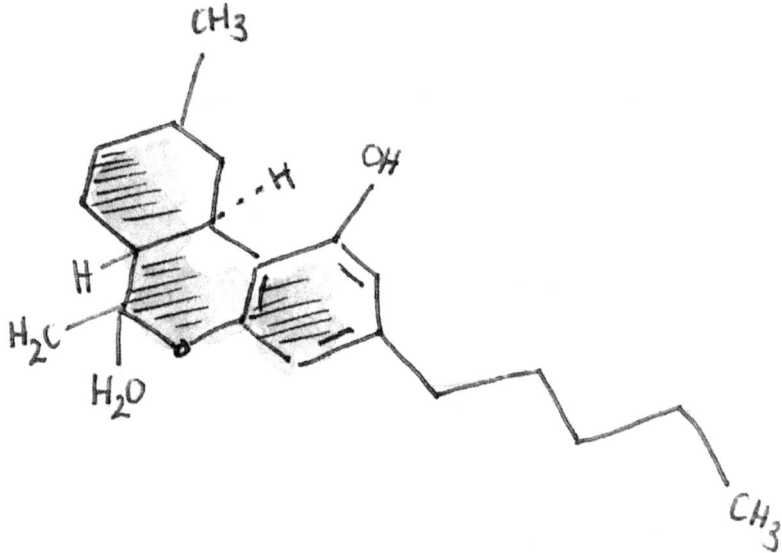

~Chemicals~

Chemical	Serotonin This chemical regulates our mood	Dopamine This chemical helps us to feel motivated, determined, and feel pleasure	Oxytocin This chemical makes us feel loved	Endorphins This chemical helps with pain
How to produce them naturally	- Exercise - Meditation - Vitamin D from the sun - Being out in nature - Healthy food consumption	- Rewarding yourself - Daily to do lists - Receiving compliments and positive feedback - Our favourite foods - Creating - Meditation	- Hug someone - Tell your loved ones that you love them - Nurture an animal or baby - Acupuncture	- Laughter - Using essential oils like lavender - Having a relaxing bath - Exercise - Meditation

~Karmic Relationships~

Some people are meant to be in our lives short term, others are meant to be here long term. Every relationship we have has purpose and for the time that it lasted in your life, it served the purpose it was meant to serve. Every relationship is there to teach you a lesson. Know when a relationship no longer serves purpose in your life and have the confidence to walk away if need be.

~Closure~

Sometimes you don't get the closure that you need to move on, making you feel stuck in that situation. The truth is, closure is within our reach despite the reactions or nonreactions of the other person involved. Closure is not easy when the person that hurt you doesn't acknowledge or take accountability for their actions. However, you don't need their reassurance to move forward, their lack of accountability is enough reassurance to know that they don't deserve a place in your life. Closure is a personal experience and you can obtain this closure within yourself. Start with understanding the situation objectively, then move towards acceptance of what IS rather than what you wanted or perceived it to be. Once you have gained this acceptance, then be dedicated to letting it go. Closure is your responsibility, no one else's.

~Listen~

Your soul already knows when something or someone is right or wrong for you. You have to learn to understand this internal dialogue that goes on when we encounter certain situations. Our body and soul will reject anything that isn't good for us, pay close attention to how certain situations and people make you feel. If something unsettles you, then listen to that warning. If something calms you, then welcome that experience.

~Suffering~

We have to accept that suffering is a very normal part of life. Often, we are taught that life should always be happy, but this theory is unrealistic. If you can welcome the suffering as well as you do happiness, then the suffering will always be a lot easier to manage. Our perspectives on suffering can really determine how we overcome these obstacles. Accepting that suffering is a natural part of our existence will enable you to accept any difficulties you may experience and therefore, create a tolerance for these difficult times.

~Just Chill~

We often contribute to psychological pain by the way we react to situations. Sometimes we can over react to certain things, personalise experiences, and become very sensitive to perceived criticism around us. This misinterpretation of our experiences can exacerbate internal pain and have a very negative impact on our mental health. Learn to be patient, learn to be understanding, learn to be objective, and what you will understand is that you don't have as many problems as you think, or the problems you do have, actually aren't as bad as what you thought they were.

~Challenge It~

Transform your problems into a challenge. Instead of fixating on the problem and drowning yourself in its negative, learn to switch into problem solving mode and transform that problem into a challenge you can overcome. Learning to flexibly manage our problems allows us to more easily overcome the problems we are presented with. For example, if the house is overwhelmingly messy, focus on completing one task each day, or if you lost your job, focus on finding a new one.

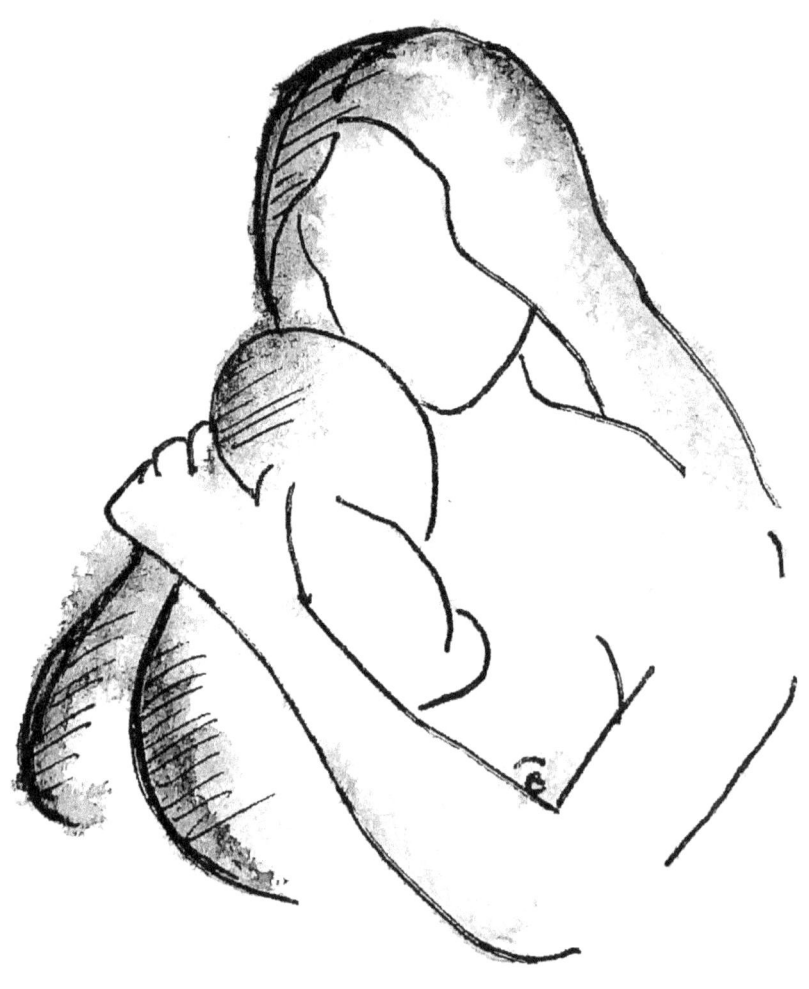

~Adulthood~

One of the aims in getting older is to slowly understand the errors in our thinking that have been modelled to us as kids. We begin to challenge our preconceived patters of understanding the world that was developed during our early life. We learn to reassess these preconceived ideas and through our life experiences, we learn what works and to shake off what doesn't work. Adulthood is unbecoming everything that no longer serves a purpose and becoming everything that you fundamentally should be.

~ Own Your Shit ~

Being a shitty person unfortunately doesn't just end with you. You then spread that shittiness on to others who then go around and spread shit on to other people... creating a continuous production line of contagious crap.

Spread love, not shit!

~ Nothing Is Solid ~

The amazing Albert Einstein demonstrated that energy and matter are so fundamentally related that they are one and the same. Subatomic refers to the parts (electrons, protons, neutrons) that make up an atom, which are building blocks of all things. Quantum physics demonstrates that every physical thing in our world is not solid and if we had a powerful instrument that looked into every little thing, you would see that atoms are actually made up of empty space; which is not solid at all but fields of energy.

- Dr. Jo Dispenza

What is even more fascinating is that this empty space varies based on the individual observing it. This is why our thoughts and perceptions are SO powerful and this is how manifestation works. You can change your life simply by changing your thoughts. Nothing is solid and there are endless opportunities for us to tap into.

~ Mental Gymnastics ~

Often people go through periods of mental gymnastics. This is the process of using coping strategies to cope with a situation that you are not satisfied with. If you are truly not happy with the situation then the coping strategies that you are using (e.g. meditation) will only be keeping you afloat, and you will constantly fall back to that uncomfortable feeling in the pit of your stomach telling you that you are not happy. This isn't because the tools you are using aren't helpful, it is because you are denying that your situation just doesn't align with what you fundamentally want. Be brave enough to walk away from something that you know deep down just isn't making you happy.

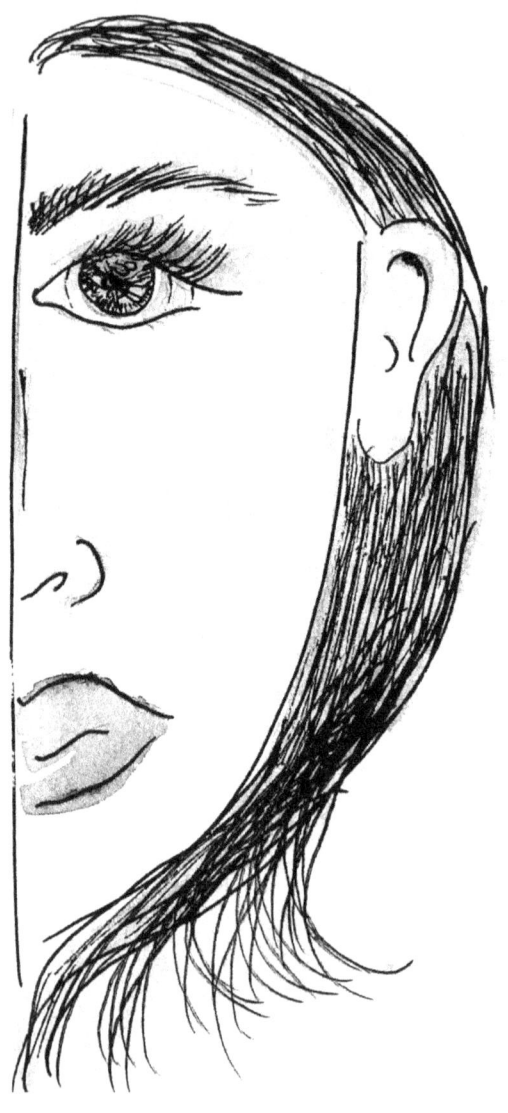

~You~

A different version of you exists in the minds of everyone that knows you.

- Luigi Pirandello

This basically means that the person you perceive yourself as actually only exists in your mind. We show different versions of ourselves to each person that we meet. If you break that down to the people in your life, your family, your friends, acquaintances and so forth, you will see that there are so many different versions of you. This is why your understanding of yourself is so important because only you will truly understand the real version of you, while everyone else's version of you is just based on different facets that you demonstrate to them. If no one is able to see all the unique and amazing facets of you, then make sure that you do

~Organised Chaos~

One of the keys to success is to be organised and have some kind of routine. When things are chaotic and disorganised it's very hard for us to accomplish things successfully. We then procrastinate and put things off due to feeling completely overwhelmed. The key is to have a routine that you can potentially stick to. Attempt to get up and go to sleep at the same time, block out time for work, family, down time, and things that you enjoy. If you have an organised routine you can somewhat follow, it makes tasks seem much more achievable.

On the next page is an example of a simplified schedule to help organise some of your chaos.

	Monday	Tuesday	Wednesday
8am			
9am			
10am			
11am			
12pm			
1pm			
2pm			
3pm			
4pm			
5pm			
6pm			
7pm			
8pm			
9pm			
10pm			
11pm			

ay	Friday	Saturday	Sunday

~ Love Prevails ~

The universe around you is completely alive, nothing is dead nor pointless; every living thing has a soul and those souls are eternal. The universe and life is organised so that all things work towards the good; everything aligns with the principle of love and it is through this language of love that every soul is guaranteed eventual happiness. Don't lose hope when you see the dysfunction in life, it will always eventually find its way back to love. The one thing I have always had full confidence in, is that love always prevails.

Acknowledgements

Thank you to Busybird Publishing for publishing my book and supporting me with its cause. I am so grateful that I had the opportunity to collaborate with a team whose energy aligns so closely with mine.

Thank you to my family and friends, I have been truly blessed with the most amazing people around me who have always believed in me and supported my crazy ventures.

More specifically…

Thank you to my dear friend Ayesha Dharmabandu for creating the illustrations for this book and bringing my words to life. We have always shared the most special bond and our values and ways of being have always aligned. I knew straight away that you would be the creativity behind this project. Thank you for being my soul sister, I love you, I appreciate you.

Thank you to my beloved Kristopher, my love for you is eternal. I am completely devoted to you and our future together. Thank you for believing in me and loving me in the most perfect of ways. Even if I said I wanted to fly to space, you would be right there next to me helping me build a rocket ship. You are amazing and I am forever grateful to have you in my life.

Mum and Dad, everything I have and everything that I am, I owe to you. Thank you for the foundation that you have provided me. It has been from this foundation that I have felt completely safe to explore life and learn about who I truly am. I can never thank you enough for loving me so unconditionally.

Disclaimer

This book is a collection of my own thoughts and is not an alternative to therapy. If you are suffering from mental health issues and require assistance then please reach out to a professional who can help you. Here is also a list of helplines that can help to direct you with that next step:

Lifeline Australia (Anyone having a personal crisis) 13 11 14

Kids Helpline (Counselling for children aged 5 to 25) 1800 55 1800

Beyond Blue (Anyone feeling anxious or depressed) 1300 224 636

MensLine Australia (Men with emotional or relationship concerns) 1300 78 99 78

Suicide Call Back Service (Anyone thinking about suicide) 1300 659 467

PANDA (Prenatal anxiety and depression Australia) 1300 726 306

QLife (support for the LGBTI community) 1800 184 527

About The Author

Maree Gatt
Clinical Psychologist & Reiki Practitioner
B.Psych, PostGrad. Dip.Psych, M.Clin.Psych

Born in the western suburbs of Melbourne, author Maree Gatt is a Clinical Psychologist and has dedicated her life to understanding and working in mental health. Maree currently runs a private practice called Peace by Piece Psychology where she works with a variety of mental health issues. Prior to moving into her own private practice, Maree has worked within many mental health settings ranging from forensic work, to drug and alcohol counselling, within various schools, and in other private practices.

Maree has always held a fascination with the universe and has dedicated many hours into understanding concepts of spirituality and consciousness. She has completed a Master level in Reiki and is a strong believer in energy healing and all that this encompasses.

Maree loves adventure and travel and from a young age she has had the urge to experience everything that life has to offer. Travel has been a big component in her life and she has had the privilege of exploring many interesting destinations.

Amongst it all, Maree has dedicated her life to helping others and it is through the platform of 'Shades of Being' that she hopes to do this on a greater scale.

Visit her website **www.pbpp.com.au**

Or follow her on Instagram **@peacebypiecepsychology**

About The Illustrator

Ayesha Dharmabandu

Ayesha Dharmabandu is a Melbourne based artist and Visual Arts teacher. She graduated with a Bachelor of Education in Creativity and the Arts; majoring in Fine Arts, Performing Arts and sub-majoring in Literature.

Ayesha is an emerging and expressive abstract artist. She has displayed her work in a number of exhibitions and is continuing to expand her artistic career. She often experiments with acrylic paints, printing, watercolour paints, graphite, ink, and gold leaf to create her works of art. Ayesha has always been inquisitive and creative, and sees art as a form of healing; a means to connect with her spirituality. Art has given her purpose. Ayesha was honoured to be asked to illustrate Maree's book, 'Shades of Being', and it has only strengthened the divine connection and bond they have.

Follow her on Instagram **@arty_aye**

www.ingramcontent.com/pod-product-compliance
Lightning Source LLC
Chambersburg PA
CBHW071519080526
44588CB00011B/1483